The Holy Spirit in Me

CAROLYN NYSTROM

Illustrated by
Wayne A. Hanna

MOODY PRESS
CHICAGO

Moody Press, a ministry of the Moody Bible Institute,
is designed for education, evangelization, and
edification. If we may assist you in knowing more about
Christ and the Christian life, please write us without
obligation: Moody Press, c/o MLM, Chicago, Illinois 60610.

Do you know the Holy Spirit?

I do. He lives in me. Let me tell you about Him.

Genesis 1:1-2

Long ago, before there was a world, God began to create. He formed the earth, a shapeless mass of muck—cold and empty and dark. But God's Spirit was moving over the waters. Soon everything in the world began to take a beautiful form. That's the way the Holy Spirit works.

After God made the world, He created people. Soon more and more people filled the earth. Fathers told their children about God, but sometimes the stories got mixed up. And some people never heard of God at all. God wanted everyone to know Him, so the Holy Spirit showed certain people what to write in a book about God. That book is the Bible. The Bible is God speaking to us.

Long after God made the world, Jesus came to earth. Just before Jesus began to teach, the Holy Spirit came down from heaven to stay with Jesus. Then God's voice sounded from heaven and said, "This is My Son; I am pleased with Him."

Ever since that time, the Holy Spirit has helped people to know Jesus.

Before I knew Jesus, I worried about bad things I'd done. But then I discovered that Jesus would forgive all of those sins—take them away forever. It was the Holy Spirit who helped me see what I had done wrong.

Even now, whenever I begin to wonder if I really do belong in God's family, the Holy Spirit helps me believe.

John 14:16-18

When Jesus was about to leave earth
and go back to His Father in heaven, His
friends felt sad. They knew they would
be lonely. But Jesus promised that the Holy
Spirit would take His place on earth. "The
Holy Spirit is *with* you, and soon He will be
in you," Jesus said. "I will never leave
you alone."

Joel 2:28-32; Acts 2:1-7

After Jesus had gone back to heaven,
His friends waited together for the Holy Spirit
to come to them. But they didn't know
exactly what would happen. Suddenly a
rushing wind filled the house. Tiny flames
of fire rested on each person, but no
one was hurt. Instead they all began to
speak in strange languages.

What do you think they talked about? You
guessed it: Jesus. Each person who stood
outside the house heard about Jesus in the
words he understood best. The Holy
Spirit had come.

Romans 12:4-8; 1 Corinthians 12:4-11; 12:27-31;
Ephesians 4:11

Along with the ability to speak in other languages, the Holy Spirit brought many other gifts to the friends of Jesus. These were not presents that they could see and touch, but special power to do God's work.

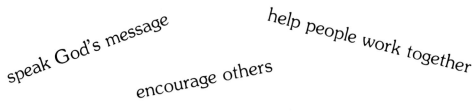

speak God's message

help people work together

encourage others

heal the sick

share

help anyone
who needs help

know when the Holy
Spirit is working

serve

bring people into
God's family

teach

speak with unknown
languages

work miracles

lead others

understand what those
words mean

kindness

knowledge

apostles

wisdom

pastors

faith

1 Corinthians 12:12-26

The Holy Spirit gave different gifts to each person because God planned for each one to do his own special job. But all the gifts helped Jesus' friends take care of each other. And together they worked for God.

Acts 3:1-10

Using the gift of healing, Peter and John made a man, too sick to walk, well enough to run and jump.

I Timothy 4:6

Using the gift of pastor, Timothy worked as leader of a new church.

Acts 16:14-15, 40

Using the gift of helps, Lydia invited Paul and his friends to stay in her home while he preached to the people of her city.

Acts 4:23-31

Using the gift of faith, a large group prayed that they would be brave enough to tell others about Jesus even if soldiers put their leaders in jail. And God made them so brave that hundreds more believed.

Ever since the day the Holy Spirit filled that room where people waited, He lives inside each person who believes in Jesus. He is God living in me. He will never leave me, and I will never leave Him.

The Bible says that our bodies are the temple of the Holy Spirit. I want my body to be a good place for God to live. So I eat the right foods. (I don't like green vegetables, but I eat them anyway.) I sleep enough to feel rested. (Sometimes that means I have to go to bed earlier than I really want to.) And I see my doctor when I'm sick. I do all that to keep my body healthy—for God.

Because the Holy Spirit is in me, He goes where I go: to school, to church, to play with my friends. He is with me at night when I wake up from a scary dream. And He helps me feel quiet and sleepy again.

I remember that when I gave myself to Jesus, Jesus gave me the Holy Spirit. And I thank Jesus.

Because the Holy Spirit goes everywhere with me, He goes some places that God would not want to go. The Holy Spirit was there the day I pulled Bobby off the swing and hit him. The Holy Spirit was there when I sat behind our house and practiced saying bad words. The Holy Spirit was there the night I said, "I don't want to pray," and turned over and went to sleep.

The Bible says, "Don't make the Holy Spirit sad."

Ezekiel 36:26-27; Romans 8:12-13

I try not to do things that make the Holy Spirit sad, but I do not have to try all by myself. The Holy Spirit helps me say no to sin.

Just yesterday, when I was playing at Bobby's house, I saw a little car on his dresser. I wanted that little car so much that I almost put it in my pocket. But I didn't. The Holy Spirit helped me not to steal.

John 14:26

The Holy Spirit helps in other ways. The Holy Spirit helps me to learn about Jesus. Sometimes He helps my Sunday school teacher tell my class an interesting Bible story. Sometimes He helps Mom answer my questions about God. Sometimes He just helps my mind understand what is hard even for grown-ups. And after that, the Holy Spirit helps me remember it all.

John 15:26-27; Acts 1:8

The Holy Spirit helps me tell others about Jesus. God wants many people in His family, and He wants me to show them how to come to Him. The Holy Spirit helps me say just the right words that would bring them to Jesus.

Acts 16:6-10

The Holy Spirit helps me to make good choices—even without my knowing it. Like the time I chose to ride my bike to the pond instead of to the woods. Later I found out that a swarm of bees had landed in the woods that day.

Ephesians 4:4-6

The Holy Spirit helps me to love other people in God's family. There's Granny Tucker, who is eighty years old and needs a wheelchair at church, and Kenny Skaggs, who is sixteen and shoots baskets with me, and Priscilla Watts, who doesn't have any family near here, but she always has Sunday dinner with us. We are in God's family together, so the Holy Spirit helps us to love each other.

Romans 8:26-27

And the Holy Spirit helps me pray. If I don't know how to pray, the Holy Spirit teaches me. Even if I don't know what to ask God for, the Holy Spirit prays for me. And God understands.

John 14:16

When you think of all those different jobs, what do you think might be another name for the Holy Spirit? That's right. The Bible calls Him the "Helper."

The Bible says that people who belong
to God are like trees. (Of course we don't look
like trees. The Bible is speaking of what
we do, not the way we look.) The tree behind
my house gives us apples every fall. It is
an apple tree, so apples are its fruit.

Just so, the Holy Spirit in us causes us to
give the fruit of the Spirit.

When I help my friends stop fighting,
when I am patient about a broken shoestring,
when I am gentle with my puppy, then I am
giving out the fruit of the Spirit. And I
am happy. So is the Spirit in me.